LILITH

Allan Havis

BROADWAY PLAY PUBLISHING INC.

357 W 20th St., NY NY 10011
212 627-1055

LILITH
© Copyright 1991 by Allan Havis

Grateful acknowledgment is given to the Epstein Family for permission to reproduce the cover artwork.

First printing: April 1991
ISBN: 0-88145-092-8

Book design: Marie Donovan
Word processing: WordMarc Composer Plus
Typographic controls: Xerox Ventura Publisher, Professional Extension
Typeface: Palatino
Printed on recycled acid-free paper and bound in the USA.

ABOUT THE AUTHOR

Allan Havis' works, which include ADORING THE MADONNA, A DARING BRIDE, THE HABIT OF LYING, and THE LADIES OF FISHER COVE, have been produced by Long Wharf, Hartford Stage, American Repertory Theater, South Coast Rep, Virginia Stage Company, The Philadelphia Theater Company, Berkshire Theater Festival, Home For the Contemporary Arts, Ensemble Studio Theater, and at the Viceroy in England. In New York, he has directed his plays at WPA, West Bank Cafe, and BACA. His libretto for the musical AMERICAN PIE will be produced at the Chichester Festival Theater in England in the spring of 1991.

Allan Havis' play MOROCCO received the 1985 FDG/CBS Award, the 1986 Playwrights USA Award from HBO, a 1987 Kennedy Center/American Express Grant, and will be presented on German Radio in 1991 by Rowohlt Theater-Verlag. Produced throughout the country, MOROCCO was published in TCG's anthology NEW PLAYS USA 3 and in a Broadway Play Publishing single-author collection along with his plays HOSPITALITY and MINK SONATA. His play HAUT GOUT was also seen on both coasts and published by TCG.

Allan Havis' children's novel ALBERT THE ASTRONOMER, published by Harper and Row, will be adapted for the stage through a commission by Sundance Institute. Other commissions have come from South Coast Rep and CSC Rep. He has been assisted by major grants from Guggenheim, NEA, Rockefeller, McKnight, and New York State Foundation for the Arts. His residencies include the Sundance Institute, the Edward Albee Foundation, the MacDowell Colony, the Wurlitzer Foundation, and a Hawthornden Fellowship in Scotland. Allan Havis is a professor at the Graduate Theater School of the University of California, San Diego, and holds an MFA from the Yale School of Drama.

LILITH was originally produced by HOME for Contemporary Theater and Art, Ltd., Randy Rollison, Artistic Director, and Parris Relkin, Managing Director. The play opened on 12 September 1990, with the following cast and creative contributors:

ADAM/ARNOLD .... Zach Grenier
LILITH/CLAIRE .... Allison Janney
VOICE (ARCHANGEL) .... Joel Rooks
EPPY .... Lindsey Margo Smith
EARL .... Carl Purcell

Director .... Robert Bailey
Set designer .... John Lee Beatty
Costume designer .... Nancy Thun
Lighting designer .... Rui Rita
Associate director .... Regina Miranda
Stage manager .... Lisa Iacucci

THE MYTH OF LILITH

Lilith, a female spirit, holds a central position
in Western demonology and Jewish mythology.
Midrashic literature expands the legend of Adam and
Eve, identifying Lilith as Adam's first wife, created
from the earth at the same time as Adam, and who,
unwilling to forgo her equality, disputed with him
the manner of their bedroom intercourse. Defiantly
pronouncing the Ineffable Name, she flew off into the
air. On Adam's request, the Almighty sent after her
three angels: Snwy, Snsnwy, and Smnglf. Finding
Lilith in the Red Sea, the angels threatened that if she
did not return, 100 of her sons would die every day.
She refused, claiming that she was expressly created
to harm newborn infants. However, she had to swear
that whenever she saw the image of those angels in
an amulet, she would lose her power over the infant.

From various ancient traditions, the image of Lilith —
dark, alluring woman's face, long hair, and the ability
to sprout wings — has two primary roles: the
strangler of children and the seducer of men,
from whose nocturnal emissions she bears an infinite
number of demonic sons. From the sixteenth century,
it was commonly believed that if an infant laughed in
his sleep it was an indication that Lilith was playing
with him, and it therefore was advisable to tap him on
the nose to avert danger. It was also believed that if a
young man slept alone in a house, Lilith would steal
his semen through the most devious means.

PRODUCTION NOTES

The playing style of LILITH demands a careful balance of humor, intelligence, and menace. The first part of the play is lighter and disarmingly amusing, compared to the horrific second part. Demons certainly do kick ass. However, there is sufficient wit and confidence behind the defensive measures taken by ARNOLD and EPPY in resisting CLAIRE. EPPY is a formidable opponent, gifted with sarcasm. It would be a mistake to make the second part unnecessarily gothic and fraught with hysteria. Imagining Strindberg as directed by Mike Nichols, Part Two flows darkly comic and unpredictably erotic (THE GRADUATE meets GHOST SONATA).

Although magic is cited in the text, please de-emphasize the weaponry of amulets and the like in order to depict psychological battles above the supernatural.

The key to realizing LILITH on stage is in her irresistible charm, irony, and her ability to seduce ARNOLD, EPPY, EARL, the Gods, and her theater audience. Moreover, in the final twilight moments, EPPY may recognize LILITH in her own image — two women with the same face, this being a far greater paradox than simply a wife fighting a beautiful invading mistress from the Garden of Eden.

For my Mother
In her many travels,
And to Helen nestled
In her Chelsea Citadel,
With love always

PART ONE: BEFORE EVE

CHARACTERS

ADAM

LILITH

VOICE (ARCHANGEL)

SETTING

Somewhere in the Garden of Eden

TIME

Creation

PART ONE

(Long pause; ADAM *begins nervously.)*

ADAM: She's late.

VOICE: Late?

ADAM: She said she'd be on time. I tell you . . . it's typical. I'm really at wit's end.

VOICE: Shall we begin?

ADAM: Yes, why not? The damn woman probably woke up on the wrong side of the bed today.

VOICE: As the counsel for these proceedings, I want to state that I take no side in the argument. Is that clear, Adam?

ADAM: Yes.

VOICE: Are you uncomfortable?

ADAM: *(Somewhat nervous)* Uncomfortable?

VOICE: Ill at ease?

ADAM: Not at all.

VOICE: You initiated this hearing — just for the record.

ADAM: For good reason!

VOICE: Would you like to begin your deposition?

ADAM: Where do I begin?

VOICE: Wherever . . .

ADAM: Our problems began . . . in bed.

VOICE: Yes?

ADAM: Should I go into detail?

VOICE: But of course.

ADAM: She cannot be pleased. And believe me,
I've tried gallantly.

VOICE: Have you discussed this with her?

ADAM: Yes, a thousand times. She demands to be on
top. Always.

VOICE: And have you tried this?

ADAM: Yes. Twice.

VOICE: How was it?

ADAM: How was it?

VOICE: Answer the question, Adam.

ADAM: It was shitty. *(Pause)* I mean. . .she really bears
down. Like a fricken' wine press. Who needs it?

VOICE: Have you told her this?

ADAM: Sure. A thousand times. She just laughs in my
face. Lilith doesn't care about anything but herself,
you understand.

VOICE: So you fight over sexual positions?

ADAM: Yes, day and night. She also criticizes the
angle of my erection. She says I'm like a dumpy little
stationwagon. She wants the goddamn sports model.
(Pause) She has an attitude, you understand.

VOICE: Have you ever hit Lilith?

ADAM: No, never.

VOICE: Are you certain?

ADAM: Yes.

VOICE: Do you love Lilith?

ADAM: I don't know. *(Silence.* LILITH *enters.)* You're late.

LILITH: Yes. I know.

ADAM: Why are you late?

LILITH: I couldn't find the right building. I'm very sorry. Is this going to take all day?

ADAM: Sit down, Lilith.

LILITH: Where is He?

ADAM: He's here. Button up. *(*LILITH *buttons her blouse.)*

VOICE: As the counsel for these proceedings, I want to state that I take no side in the argument. Is that clear, Lilith?

LILITH: *(Squinting to see the voice)* Yes, your Honor.

VOICE: We began with Adam's deposition.

LILITH: Is all this really necessary?

ADAM: Yes, damnit!

LILITH: I've been very good to this man, your Honor.

VOICE: Adam states that you take the missionary position. Is this true?

LILITH: Yes, otherwise I get nosebleeds.

ADAM: She's lying.

VOICE: Are you lying, Lilith?

LILITH: Yes.

VOICE: Adam is supposed to have the missionary position.

LILITH: Because he's a man?

VOICE: Yes, Lilith.

LILITH: But that's ridiculous. Where is it written?

VOICE: Lilith, you are supposed to obey your husband.

LILITH: My husband is neurotic.

ADAM: That's irrelevant.

LILITH: Don't contradict me, Adam. You're neurotic because you have no role model.

ADAM: Insolence morning, noon, and night.

LILITH: What do you expect, roses and champagne?

ADAM: It's the Creator's fault.

LILITH: So you keep saying.

ADAM: We came at the same time. It's all about timing, don't you understand?

LILITH: Why should you precede me?

ADAM: Because I'm man.

LILITH: You're a wimp.

VOICE: Who said the Ineffable Name?

LILITH: What?

VOICE: The Ineffable Name?

ADAM: She did.

LILITH: *(Hitting* ADAM *in the arm)* Snitch!

VOICE: Lilith . . .

LILITH: *(Sweetly)* Yes?

VOICE: This is your deposition.

LILITH: Okay. It's true. I said the Ineffable.

VOICE: Why, Lilith?

LILITH: Because I was pissed off.

VOICE: Explain.

LILITH: Because the Creator favors my husband.

VOICE: That is untrue.

LILITH: Then why did I lose my children?

VOICE: Because you abandoned your lawful husband.

LILITH: Unjust.

VOICE: You came to Earth to give emotional comfort to Adam.

LILITH: I am not a kitchen appliance.

VOICE: Shall I put that in your deposition.

LILITH: Please.

ADAM: *(An aside)* You're not getting on their good side, dearest.

LILITH: Sycophant.

ADAM: Succubus.

LILITH: Take that back.

ADAM: No. It goes into the deposition.

LILITH: You've never loved me.

ADAM: I have loved you like no other.

LILITH: And Eve?

ADAM: Who?

LILITH: She's on the drawing board, you ninny.

VOICE: Enough, Lilith.

LILITH: I know what's coming.

VOICE: How do you know?

LILITH: I have my sources.

VOICE: This is very damaging to your interests.

LILITH: I'm not demonic. I don't care what the tabloids say.

VOICE: We're getting off track.

ADAM: May I read from the archives?

LILITH: Not that filth, darling.

ADAM: These are authorized notes from the archives. *(Coughs, clears throat, reads)* The creation of woman: *(Pause)* Don't make her from the head of man, lest she carry her head high in arrogance; not from the eye, lest she be wanton-eyed; not from the ear, lest she be an eavesdropper; not from the mouth, lest she be a chatterbox; find a chaste portion of the body. *(Pause. Smiling.)* From the rib. Chaste and subordinate.

LILITH: Impossible.

ADAM: I don't make the rules.

LILITH: But you make the legends.

ADAM: No, darling.

LILITH: Did we come out of the Creator's nostrils?

ADAM: And if we had?

LILITH: We came out at the very same moment.

ADAM: And if we came from the dust in the canyon?

LILITH: We appeared simultaneously.

ADAM: And if that were true?

LILITH: It means we have equality.

ADAM: We do.

LILITH: Why can't I have the missionary position?

ADAM: I'm not a whipping horse, Lilith.

LILITH: I want my pleasure, darling, any way I can.

ADAM: Not at my expense.

LILITH: You're seriously limited, darling.

ADAM: Perhaps I am.

VOICE: Is there a decision between you?

ADAM: A decision?

VOICE: You've asked for a separation.

ADAM: Yes, in anger.

VOICE: Your deposition.

ADAM: She makes me feel guilty.

VOICE: Why?

ADAM: Because I crave her at night.

VOICE: How do you crave her?

ADAM: Like a whore.

LILITH: So?

ADAM: I think it's wrong. But she eggs me on.

LILITH: Liar.

ADAM: A lightning bolt should drop down. . . .

LILITH: The next woman will be duller than you.

ADAM: Better than a she-demon.

LILITH: Because I sprout wings at night?

ADAM: Don't make a joke of it.

LILITH: Why not?

ADAM: This is not the place for jokes.

LILITH: I don't want a separation.

ADAM: I do.

LILITH: I'll utter the name. . . .

ADAM: Don't.

VOICE: Lilith.

LILITH: You cut my hair to shreds.

VOICE: An improvement.

LILITH: You stole my wings.

VOICE: Our mistake.

LILITH: No. I think not.

VOICE: Now you resemble Adam.

LILITH: I have a woman's face. I don't look like Adam.

VOICE: Give him back his semen.

LILITH: *(Visibly puzzled)* What?

VOICE: He feels melancholic.

LILITH: He cries each week. What can you expect?

ADAM: She wants mirrors in our bedroom.

VOICE: Mirrors?

ADAM: On the ceiling.

VOICE: Lilith . . .

LILITH: Yes?

VOICE: Mirrors are a bad idea.

ADAM: See?

LILITH: I'm not taking them down.

VOICE: Mirrors will go in the deposition. Petty vanity.

LILITH: Go on, banish me. You don't like my appetite nor my humor.

ADAM: For the record, she is an honest soul.

LILITH: I want my babies returned.

ADAM: These creatures are not babies.

LILITH: They're your babies too.

ADAM: I don't care.

LILITH: A hundred babies at the Red Sea, bathing.

ADAM: *(To* VOICE*)* I don't want custody of them.

VOICE: Lilith, they cannot be returned.

LILITH: Why not?

VOICE: You can never see them again. You can never spawn more winged children. This is an edict.

LILITH: *(To* ADAM*)* You made them do this.

ADAM: No, darling.

LILITH: I curse your children with the next woman.

ADAM: There's no other woman, Lilith.

LILITH: I will petition Heaven.

ADAM: And go fight City Hall.

LILITH: Have your divorce, Adam. I've lost my audience with these demented angels.

VOICE: A sharp tongue hurts your image.

LILITH: Is this a free consultation, or are we paying by the hour?

VOICE: There's property to be divided. Adam?

ADAM: Yes, I . . . want the garden.

VOICE: Lilith?

LILITH: *(Quietly angry)* I heard him.

VOICE: Do you contest that?

LILITH: He can keep the garden.

ADAM: Thank you.

LILITH: You may weed and roam the land. It was never really mine. Hump like a doggy. The world was given to you. I'll fly with my demon friends.

ADAM: That's a bad idea.

VOICE: Lilith.

LILITH: What?

VOICE: You mustn't hurt Adam's children.

LILITH: I made no threats.

VOICE: You are capable of anything.

LILITH: And so are you.

VOICE: Is your deposition completed?

LILITH: No.

ADAM: She plans to argue.

LILITH: I know the new woman. I am indignant.
She will clean your soiled clothes. Will bend down
for you. Will remain silent and empty-headed. She
will misbehave in her dreams. A cowardly woman.
(*Looking directly at* ADAM) But you'll feel superior by
her side.

ADAM: Calm down, sweetheart.

LILITH: The angels will descend and take me away.

VOICE: Because you said the Ineffable.

LILITH: Do you blame me?

VOICE: You were supposed to return immediately.

LILITH: I am the first woman. Adam will never forget
me.

ADAM: It's true. I see two women in my sleep.

LILITH: I prefer punishment to living with this
imperfect man.

ADAM: Do you?

LILITH: Your stupidity is more wicked than all of me.

ADAM: Why can't you flatter me just once?

LILITH: I fear it would arouse you.

VOICE: Lilith, you're the only woman alive.

LILITH: Do I get a statue?

VOICE: Yes. In all probability.

LILITH: Wonderful.

VOICE: What else do you request?

LILITH: Another man.

VOICE: There is only Adam in the garden.

LILITH: Surely if he can be given Eve, I merit someone.

VOICE: You are the only woman.

LILITH: We all know there's someone else. Do what you want with me. This proceeding is useless. I don't know why you forced me to show up for this. Who are we fooling?

ADAM: You may want partial support.

LILITH: From you?

ADAM: Yes.

LILITH: I don't want such gestures.

ADAM: You're still my wife.

LILITH: Then I want another child.

VOICE: With wings?

LILITH: Yes. Why not?

VOICE: It's an affront.

LILITH: You're being hysterical.

VOICE: No more children, Lilith.

LILITH: Then why was I put here?

ADAM: Domestic bliss. You really ought to compromise. It's not difficult. *(Inadvertent irony)* After all, look at the compromises I've made.

LILITH: Adam, either you want me or you don't.

VOICE: *(Pause)* Adam . . .

ADAM: Perhaps if you were gagged.

LILITH: Gagged?

ADAM: From time to time.

LILITH: You're a pigeon-headed misogynist.

ADAM: Nonsense.

LILITH: You envy my freedom, and call me a demon. I won't budge without my children.

ADAM: Lilith, you know that's impossible. *(Pause)* The angels have destroyed every unacceptable child.

LILITH: Is this true?

VOICE: Yes.

LILITH: The children were our children.

ADAM: I know.

LILITH: I'm in tremendous pain.

ADAM: Yes, I know.

LILITH: I'm being cheated.

ADAM: Take the garden. I'll move on.

LILITH: You prefer suburbia.

ADAM: What?

LILITH: The garden will become suburbia.

VOICE: Lilith. Adam is willing to offer you a proposition.

ADAM: I am?

VOICE: Yes.

ADAM: *(Touching* LILITH's *arm)* Listen carefully.

VOICE: If you wear a longer robe which covers your legs and arms, if you will never assume the missionary position in bed, if you wear the blindfold and gag. . . .

LILITH: To hell with your offer.

ADAM: He's not through yet. . . .

VOICE: If you promise never to utter the Ineffable Name. . . .

LILITH: I cannot promise you these things.

ADAM: *(To* LILITH, *quietly)* Why can't you please us?

LILITH: I don't know. *(Pause)* I want to meet the other woman.

ADAM: Why?

LILITH: Curiosity.

ADAM: You say the most annoying things.

LILITH: May I have a moment alone?

ADAM: Now?

LILITH: Yes. *(Pause)* Have a beer.

ADAM: *(Exits)* Alright.

VOICE: You have my sympathies, Lilith.

LILITH: I'll return to the Red Sea tonight.

VOICE: As you wish.

LILITH: I don't trust Adam.

VOICE: Adam feels the same.

LILITH: I have no partner in life.

VOICE: An ox knows his master.

LILITH: An ox is an animal.

VOICE: Lilith, perhaps you wear too much mascara.

LILITH: Too much?

VOICE: Such dark forbidding eyes. . .

LILITH: Thank you.

VOICE: You're quite a beauty.

LILITH: Does Adam find me beautiful?

VOICE: Yes. Exceedingly.

LILITH: Do you?

VOICE: Yes.

LILITH: Is my mouth round?

VOICE: Round and most excellent.

LILITH: And my breasts?

VOICE: Rather delightful, Lilith.

LILITH: An ox knows his master.

VOICE: It's an interpretation.

LILITH: You're an interpreter?

VOICE: Yes.

LILITH: *(Stretches out arms like wings)* Do you see arms?

VOICE: No.

LILITH: What do you see?

VOICE: Demon wings.

LILITH: Do you see my private parts too?

VOICE: Yes.

LILITH: Are you excited?

VOICE: I'm on duty.

LILITH: Give Adam wings.

VOICE: Adam has legs.

LILITH: Why make us so different?

VOICE: It just happened that way.

LILITH: No. Impossible.

VOICE: Lilith . . .

LILITH: You made me too clever.

VOICE: As clever as Adam.

LILITH: Adam's neurotic.

VOICE: Not terribly.

LILITH: He needs a mother. A psychiatrist. A better tailor.

VOICE: Perhaps.

LILITH: The other woman. . .is my enemy.

VOICE: The other woman is still you.

LILITH: Pinned under Adam's torso? I want to meet Eve.

VOICE: If that is arranged, will you return the favor?

LILITH: That depends.

VOICE: Trust us a bit.

LILITH: Alright.

VOICE: Shut your eyes.

LILITH: Why?

VOICE: Lilith . . . *(She shuts her eyes.)* Keep them shut.

LILITH: Is that her?

VOICE: More or less.

LILITH: *(Eyes open)* How pathetic!

VOICE: Do you really think so?

(ADAM *enters*.)

ADAM: Well?

LILITH: I'm disgusted.

ADAM: How about lunch?

LILITH: You're getting the shaft.

ADAM: Am I?

VOICE: Adam, you may have to prepare an amulet.

ADAM: An amulet?

VOICE: A lucky charm.

ADAM: Is the deposition completed?

VOICE: Yes.

ADAM: Lilith?

LILITH: What?

ADAM: Are you upset with me?

LILITH: No.

ADAM: Should I believe you?

LILITH: No.

ADAM: I want to do what's best for both.

LILITH: How easily you deceive yourself.

ADAM: And you don't?

LILITH: If I deceive myself, it's without malice to you.
If I deceive you, it's out of kindness.

ADAM: I want to believe you, Lilith. I really do.

LILITH: This woman Eve will introduce you to sin.

ADAM: Sin?

LILITH: Evil. She acts unconscious. That's evil.

ADAM: Evil.

LILITH: Wake up, Adam.

ADAM: Who is this. . .Eve?

LILITH: She's a woman with half a brain.

VOICE: Untrue.

LILITH: Eve is a cipher. How vulnerable they
will be together. Two waifs in exile.

ADAM: I'm not an imbecile, darling. You
underestimate me. Does this Eve take the
upper or lower position?

LILITH: You get the missionary.

ADAM: Is she as sexy as you?

LILITH: She has a vagina, Adam.

ADAM: You seem bitter.

LILITH: I am.

ADAM: Does she keep kosher?

LILITH: Do you?

ADAM: No cheeseburgers.

LILITH: No oral sex.

ADAM: No kidding? What about Montessori training?

LILITH: Ask her.

ADAM: Are we divorced?

LILITH: I think so.

ADAM: It feels quite odd, Lilith. Have we done the
right thing?

LILITH: No.

ADAM: Do you still love me?

LILITH: Perhaps.

ADAM: Other men will come along.

LILITH: Adam, my punishment begins now.

ADAM: What punishment?

LILITH: I'm going back to the Red Sea.

ADAM: Alone?

LILITH: With the three angels.

ADAM: In bondage?

LILITH: Probably.

ADAM: And your wings?

LILITH: They will try some surgery.

ADAM: Surgery is painful.

LILITH: You can be very sincere, Adam.

ADAM: At least I can stay with you until. . . .

LILITH: No.

ADAM: Why do I need an amulet?

LILITH: For protection.

ADAM: From whom?

LILITH: From me.

ADAM: Why?

LILITH: Because I tickle little boys in their sleep.

ADAM: What little boys?

LILITH: All the little boys in their cribs. Come,
the day's over. We should walk.

ADAM: I'm very tired.

LILITH: There, give me your shoulder. *(She takes his
shoulders in hand.)* You've gotten broader. Nice round
arms. Strong arms. We need affection. Why do we
need so much affection?

ADAM: *(Directions for massage)* To the left. That's it.

LILITH: I feel the heat leave your skin.

ADAM: I feel your fingernails.

LILITH: Shall I stop?

ADAM: No.

LILITH: Reject this other woman.

ADAM: I haven't even met her.

LILITH: Her stupidity will tempt the serpent.

ADAM: I believe the angels will keep vigil.

LILITH: And the serpent will enter her.

ADAM: Impossible.

LILITH: And then she will be worse than me.

ADAM: The serpent would have to kill me first.

LILITH: All bets are on the serpent.

ADAM: How do you know so much about her?

LILITH: I have awareness.

ADAM: *(He holds her hands from over his shoulder.)* Yes, I know you do.

LILITH: Take me to bed, Adam.

ADAM: Now?

LILITH: Please.

ADAM: Why now?

LILITH: I believe in great gestures.

ADAM: You won't break down my resistance.

LILITH: A moment in bed. That's all.

ADAM: Angels may come.

LILITH: Not this moment.

ADAM: So brazen, Lilith.

LILITH: It must be your cologne.

ADAM: Our marriage has ended.

LILITH: One more time, Adam.

ADAM: I fear the angels.

LILITH: You should fear me more.

ADAM: Don't take advantage of the situation.

LILITH: I want one more child.

ADAM: No, it is forbidden.

LILITH: Don't make me any lonelier. I'll go crazy, Adam.

ADAM: Please.

LILITH: I'll take the bottom position, darling.

ADAM: Oh?

LILITH: It's a rare occasion.

ADAM: I suppose it is.

LILITH: If you wait too long I'll withdraw the offer.

ADAM: You know how to negotiate.

LILITH: Survivor skills. *(Kisses* ADAM *on the neck, seductively.* ADAM *mounts her awkwardly, excitedly.)* One learns such skills quickly.

ADAM: I can't resist very well.

LILITH: Splendid.

VOICE: *(Abruptly)* I think discretion is in order, Adam.

ADAM: *(Sheepishly, escaping love's embrace)* Yes, of course.

VOICE: I needn't lecture here.

ADAM: It was our way of parting.

VOICE: A short memory will hurt you.

ADAM: I've a long memory all in all.

VOICE: Lilith, leave him be. *(A faint bell is heard in the distance.)*

LILITH: Is she here?

VOICE: Yes.

LILITH: Adam.

ADAM: What?

LILITH: I wish you had guts.

ADAM: It wouldn't change a thing.

LILITH: You need to let out a fine scream.

ADAM: Like one of yours?

LILITH: Like mine.

ADAM: Then I would be banished.

LILITH: Either way you will be banished.

ADAM: Why do you say such things?

LILITH: Adam, it's still not too late. Take the missionary position. *(She strides over* ADAM, *like a horse.)* Or I will.

ADAM: Down, Lilith.

LILITH: No.

ADAM: Don't make me raise my voice.

LILITH: Go ahead. Raise hell.

ADAM: Your behavior's in poor taste.

LILITH: The angels have gone to lunch. Now.

ADAM: I'll wait for the next woman.

LILITH: The last time's the hottest, Adam.
(Arms outstretched) These aren't arms, these are

wings of a great spirit. Before Eve there was neither
innocence nor sin. Lose me, you'll never get a second
chance.

ADAM: Stop moving about.

LILITH: It is a dance for you, sweetheart.

ADAM: You tease me like a child.

LILITH: Take down your clothes.

ADAM: No.

LILITH: Or take mine.

ADAM: The angels will torture us.

LILITH: I have an amulet against them. See?

ADAM: Put that thing away.

LILITH: Rub it between your thighs, Adam.

ADAM: I hate these perfumes of yours.

LILITH: You needn't put on more than a droplet.

ADAM: *(Near his nose, he smells vial.)* It's awful.

LILITH: So are the angels overhead.

ADAM: And this will keep them away?

LILITH: Like smoke to mosquitoes.

ADAM: But they will know.

LILITH: They only know jealousy.

ADAM: If you have another child, the angels will exact
a cost on you.

LILITH: I'll assume that responsibility. *(Hands over vial)*
Here, Adam. Seize the moment.

ADAM: I won't handle it. You put it on me.

LILITH: Alright.

ADAM: Quickly.

LILITH: *(Embracing him from behind, she rubs the contents of the vial around his legs.)* Be still.

ADAM: You're tickling me.

LILITH: Almost done. *(Puts vial away)* Give me your hand.

ADAM: *(Obliging)* Now what?

LILITH: Caress me. You know where. *(They embrace. His hand slips to her abdomen.)* The angels are away. See?

ADAM: Darling, you've lost some weight here.

LILITH: From anxiety.

ADAM: I'm having trouble.

LILITH: Trouble?

ADAM: My hand can't go inside.

LILITH: Adam . . .

ADAM: Really, dear. Something's clogged.

LILITH: Push.

ADAM: Damn it, I am.

LILITH: Adam . . .

ADAM: You've been sewn up.

LILITH: *(Her hand reaches down to check.)* Sewn up?

ADAM: From side to side. Who did this?

LILITH: Our last indignity. I can't take it anymore. Hold me as tight as you can. Think of another opening inside me. Take me, Adam. You can still take me completely. *(ADAM begins to shake in coitus.)* Don't be weak. Don't break your concentration. I know you're in pain. Soon it will be over. *(He seems disabled and weak-kneed.)* Adam, you can penetrate me now. One more moment to climb. One more loving caress. One more kiss. One more whisper. One more second. Now. *(ADAM falls to his knees, exhausted and in shock.)* Such valor, Adam. Such human authority. Such locomotion.

ADAM: I'm damaged for life.

LILITH: Nonsense. Your foreskin is intact. If you want, I can make a simple splint. That should hold you well.

ADAM: *(Loud galloping horses are heard.)* Do you hear the angels coming?

LILITH: No.

ADAM: They're bringing the new woman.

LILITH: They're bringing surgical equipment, Adam. *(Pause)* They will cut open our flesh. My ovaries, your rib cage. They will give you signs of age, too. Your stomach will roll, your jowls will fall, your mind will wither. *(Pause)* I thought you were impossible to live with. But I still honor you. I do. You show kindness at the oddest of times. You and I should have the same strength of mind. Really, my complaint is no more than this. *(Caressing ADAM's hair)* I'm not responsible for things I might do later. You may curse me. I know Eve will. You'll have much to explain. You best forget everything, Adam. Get drunk. Or they will put you to sleep like a fragile cub.

VOICE: Pardon this interruption.

LILITH: *(Kissing ADAM tenderly on the neck)* It's happy hour.

VOICE: Adam, either you want this woman . . . or not.

ADAM: I'm very confused.

VOICE: Very well then. Can you find the sack under the brush?

ADAM: Over there?

VOICE: Yes, Adam.

ADAM: *(Crossing over)* What do I do?

VOICE: Open the sack.

ADAM: *(Opens it)* Now what?

VOICE: Take out the cord. *(ADAM obeys.)* Bind her legs and hands.

ADAM: Why?

VOICE: Do it, Adam. We've run out of patience.

ADAM: You mustn't harm her.

VOICE: Do it, Adam. Or she will bind you.

ADAM: *(Obeying)* Well, I think this is rather unnecessary.

LILITH: Tell Eve to live with paranoia.

ADAM: Right.

VOICE: Now take out the cloth and gag her.

LILITH: How utterly primitive.

VOICE: Orders are orders.

ADAM: This is very awkward for me.

VOICE: Do it, Adam.

ADAM: No.

VOICE: Insolence is a disease. Don't catch it.

LILITH: Sloganeer.

VOICE: Either gag her, or we drug her.

ADAM: *(Obeying)* I'm sorry, darling.

VOICE: Tightly.

ADAM: Forgive me, Lilith. *(Tugging for extra measure)* Now what?

VOICE: Apologize to the Creator.

ADAM: Apologize for what?

VOICE: For fornicating with an unmarried woman.

ADAM: I apologize with an explanation.

VOICE: No explanations.

ADAM: That was no unmarried woman.

VOICE: Now she's pregnant, Adam. *(Pause)* Do you realize the consequences?

ADAM: Lilith's pregnant?

VOICE: You're a bungler, Adam.

ADAM: So I am.

VOICE: We're sending Lilith far, far away.

ADAM: Where?

LILITH: *(Heard under her gag)* A prison in New Jersey.

ADAM: For how long?

VOICE: Until she's rehabilitated.

ADAM: I don't mean to seem cynical, but do you really think that will help her?

VOICE: Yes. If we leave her in the desert, she'll sprout a new pair of wings. If we drop her in the Red Sea, she'll grow fins. She bequeathed the garden to you. Which leaves us few choices.

ADAM: What about the expectancy?

VOICE: The angels are in conference.

ADAM: It will be my child, too.

VOICE: No, Adam. This child, like the others, will carry her traits. They will rail against Heaven, throwing stones and blue words at the angels. They will frolic in the night. Cause mayhem in the Creator's

world. Be more faithful to Lilith than to the Creator.
(Pause) You are our man in the garden. Our
authorized representative on two legs. A pedestrian,
a patriarch, a parrot of our special liking.

ADAM: And this woman . . . Eve?

VOICE: More dutiful than this creature.

ADAM: And if I should miss her?

VOICE: You will be happier than ever, Adam.

ADAM: Should I trust myself?

VOICE: Yes, Adam. Trust your obedience.

ADAM: I feel shameful.

VOICE: Because your organ hurts?

ADAM: Yes.

VOICE: It will bleed for three days.

ADAM: And then?

VOICE: You will be prepared for Eve. And her
intimacy. You must always be on the alert for your
first bride, Adam. She can find ways to get messages
to you. She can disrupt your serenity with Eve.
Far worse, she may claim your male offspring from
this moment on. Should she ever evade our angels in
prison, you will have to fend for yourself. Do I make
this clear?

ADAM: Yes.

VOICE: You must fear this woman more than at any
time in your memory. You brought her up for marital
review. You were the plaintiff. You were the injured
party. We have served you fair judgment. We
guarantee nothing. To give you companionship,
we make this final redraft. Know Eve. She is Lilith

without fire. Here, you may not be intimidated by
a galloping missionary.

ADAM: But my guilt.

VOICE: Your guilt? After some sleep, you won't recall
any guilt.

ADAM: I will.

VOICE: We will give you medication, Adam.

ADAM: Eve should meet Lilith first.

VOICE: Do you send the rabbit to the cobra? Look
hard at her.

ADAM: Lilith was never given enough love from
above.

VOICE: She never loved us either.

ADAM: Who gave her wings?

VOICE: It was an accident. We almost gave you a tail,
a curved spine, and an accordion. In Creation, things
are sometimes beyond expectation. In the sack, Adam,
is your medication. It's time to take it. *(Pause)* It will
make you feel better. Sit and take comfort. (ADAM
obeys.) When you awake, you will feel some pressure
in your lower chest. Think nothing of it. When you
awake, you will remember nothing but a vague joy
about women. The heat in your loins will stay aglow.
When you awake, Adam, you will thank every
bald-headed angel in Creation. (ADAM *drops,
unconscious.)* Lilith, please hear me well. We will try to
abort this child. Like you, it has wings. If you punish
us for this, we will declare war upon you. You may
claim the New Moon and all the rivers which flow
against the East. You may covet every infant newly
born to Adam henceforth. In prison you will have
freedom to come and go at daybreak. In the evening
we will contain you. Because of your great strength,

we fear you. You are, after all, like us. We will warn
every mother to watch their children carefully.
You were an accident of femininity, witchcraft,
and maternity. The Creator is sorry for His mistakes.
(Pause) You may keep your wings and fine hair.
From a good distance, you may still please Heaven's
gaze. To destroy you now would be an even greater
mistake. We take great pleasure in containing you.
Even if your belly swells, we have sealed every door.
Such is the dark blessing you will come to receive.
(Pause) The bonds are untied. You may spread your
wings.

(Slowly LILITH *lifts her arms. Her legs spread eagle,
dropping her calves at the knee. Blackout.)*

END OF PART ONE

PART TWO: AGUNAH
(BOUND WOMAN)

CHARACTERS

CLAIRE, mid-30s, attractive
EPPY, mid-30s, attractive
ARNOLD/ADAM, 40, average looks
EARL, 10, perhaps chubby

SETTING

Several locations throughout New York City: a café,
a park, EPPY and ARNOLD's apartment, CLAIRE's
apartment

TIME

The present. Autumn.
Action over two weeks.

PART TWO

SCENE ONE

(Day one. Afternoon at a chic self-service café.
CLAIRE *approaches* EPPY's *table and sits.)*

CLAIRE: I know him. Arnold. Your husband. He
works downtown with a large law firm. He was
made partner last year. My name is Claire.

EPPY: How do you know my husband?

CLAIRE: Let me buy you a drink.

EPPY: I have a headache.

CLAIRE: *(Removing various aspirin bottles)* Advil?
Tylenol? Bufferin?

EPPY: No thank you.

CLAIRE: I want to ask a favor, Eppy.

EPPY: What sort of favor?

CLAIRE: You make a beautiful wife. Radiant.
Gracious. Dainty. You must shine for Arnold. Arnold
dominates you. You know that feeling. I see it in
your lovely face. Your quiet oddness. Your need for
secrecy. You let him do this to you. You prostrated
yourself willingly. You kowtow. You indulge him in
bed. I know you do.

EPPY: I despise rude cranks.

CLAIRE: At this restaurant . . . conversations run the gamut.

EPPY: What is it that you want?

CLAIRE: I want to possess your dimwitted husband, Eppy.

EPPY: What?

CLAIRE: Own him for a solid year.

EPPY: Who are you?

CLAIRE: An unemployed ornithologist. But I live off a trust fund. It helps tremendously. I must be with Arnold for a time. I've missed him. I know his future. There will be blood in his urine.

EPPY: This is plain crazy talk.

CLAIRE: I know. Forgive me. I make poor first impressions. I shouldn't be so forward. But you must give me your husband. Just for one day then.

EPPY: Whatever for?

CLAIRE: For my amusement. For my survival.

EPPY: There are many eligible men out in the world.

CLAIRE: Arnold is different.

EPPY: In what way?

CLAIRE: His stupidity charms me to no end.

EPPY: You're very embarrassing.

CLAIRE: Yes, it's true. Embarrassment alienates men and women equally. Still, my heart is in the right place. If you only knew the things which pass for concern. I don't like pain. Makes me violent.

EPPY: What does?

CLAIRE: Pain. But you needn't worry. Since I found a new faith. God bless us all. We need God's blessings, Eppy.

EPPY: Do we?

CLAIRE: As we need a dependable man. A woman left to her own resources can never replace her ties with a single man. I read that in a magazine somewhere. And I clipped the article. Would you like to see it? It might be from *Reader's Digest*. It's about a man who will go to great lengths for love.

EPPY: What has that to do with Arnold?

CLAIRE: Don't deprive him of an affair. It's selfish. It's cruel.

EPPY: You expect me to be amused by this?

CLAIRE: No.

EPPY: Who are you, really?

CLAIRE: I'm a lonely person. Arnold won't change my world. I doubt that his leaving would change yours. He can make a decision about this . . . and by all means, let him discuss it with you.

EPPY: Claire, you must have some awareness about what you're saying. . . .

CLAIRE: Of course.

EPPY: And if I were to say that I desired your husband. . . .

CLAIRE: I would be utterly speechless.

EPPY: Because adultery stings.

CLAIRE: Indeed. To the very marrow.

EPPY: Yet you keep eyeing me.

CLAIRE: For agreement. Yes. Humor me.

EPPY: Take Arnold. For a day.

CLAIRE: With your blessings?

EPPY: I'll introduce you.

CLAIRE: As a friend from high school. As an alibi.

EPPY: Tell him whatever you want. I will say nothing.

CLAIRE: Tell me, Eppy. . . what is the taste of his mouth?

EPPY: Evergreen mint and mountain ale.

CLAIRE: In the early morning?

EPPY: In the early morning, Arnold snores.

CLAIRE: And how is his digestion?

EPPY: Very entertaining.

CLAIRE: And his private parts?

EPPY: Well, that is your last concern with Arnold. He takes good care of his private parts. Good care.

CLAIRE: Do you wash him?

EPPY: Years ago. Like a sexual ritual. I was happier then.

CLAIRE: I like your smile.

EPPY: Thank you.

CLAIRE: How old are you, Eppy?

EPPY: Thirty-five.

CLAIRE: You look very good for your age. Much healthier than myself. I envy you. Can you fault me for that?

EPPY: No.

CLAIRE: Do you have a child?

EPPY: Yes. A boy.

CLAIRE: He giggles at night.

EPPY: Yes.

CLAIRE: I make him giggle.

EPPY: Do you?

CLAIRE: I stroke his boyish nose.

EPPY: And how do you manage this?

CLAIRE: Fingers like soft ostrich feathers. Fingers which celebrate the male anatomy. Fingers which have befallen me.

EPPY: Have you no children of your own?

CLAIRE: No.

EPPY: You really ought to.

CLAIRE: Have children?

EPPY: Yes, Claire.

CLAIRE: Children like your child?

EPPY: Children are all the same.

CLAIRE: I crave winged children, Eppy. Gnomelike little bats. For an MTV special.

EPPY: That's silly.

CLAIRE: Yes.

EPPY: Children are all the same. Sweet . . . simple . . . serene.

CLAIRE: Who steals these children?

EPPY: I don't know.

CLAIRE: They seem to disappear between the bus and school. Always on the red milk cartons. Pictures on the line at the supermarket. It's so sad.

EPPY: Indeed.

CLAIRE: Something should be done.

EPPY: More police.

CLAIRE: Yes.

EPPY: Fingerprint identification.

CLAIRE: Immediately.

EPPY: It makes me so angry.

CLAIRE: Where is your little boy now?

EPPY: With Arnold.

CLAIRE: I can meet both of them? It would please me so.

EPPY: They may be out late.

CLAIRE: I'll come back then. How wonderful to meet them. And take a photograph. Or a lock of hair. How wonderful to wait for them. Waiting for Arnold after so many business trips out of town.

EPPY: Each day without Arnold makes me lonely. I know how to wait for him. Finding him at the door at seven. Leading him to bed. I can't imagine a life without him.

CLAIRE: He must love you terribly.

EPPY: Yes.

CLAIRE: An ideal couple.

EPPY: Hardly ideal.

CLAIRE: At least in my eyes. Touching the corners of my greenest envy. All I can ask is just one day with lovely Arnold. Before you change your mind, grant me your approval. I'll take him out of town. We'll wear strange clothes and sunglasses. Our names will be concealed. Please, dear Eppy. Won't you give me your consent?

EPPY: And what do I get in return?

CLAIRE: In return? You get my friendship.

EPPY: You have the oddest smile, Claire.

CLAIRE: It's my father's smile.

EPPY: How am I supposed to trust you?

CLAIRE: Is there something I can do to prove myself, Eppy?

EPPY: You seem invulnerable.

CLAIRE: Yes, I know what you mean.

EPPY: You know too much about my life. What do I know about you? What makes you make these unusual requests? Why do you show such interest in my husband and son?

CLAIRE: I've lost my husband in the war.

EPPY: I'm sorry.

CLAIRE: It's something I have trouble mentioning.

EPPY: I'm very sorry.

CLAIRE: After my husband's death, it was painful to see other men. For many years. No matter which man I find. Yet married men hold a certain fascination to me. There is a special kind of shield, Eppy, to a married man. A secure sense of belonging. A homing instinct. A willingness to father children. A momentary tenderness to family. Can one blame me for this little obsession? A forgivable indulgence. I'm losing the bloom of my youth. I'm ready for one last fling.

EPPY: Arnold is not a stud.

CLAIRE: I realize.

EPPY: You fantasize too much, Claire. My life was once like that. Life is too rude for fantasies. You mistake Arnold for some other man. He's a good husband. A good father. Faithful and modest. God-fearing. It's not Arnold you want.

CLAIRE: What's your son's name?

EPPY: Earl.

CLAIRE: How did you name him?

EPPY: Arnold and I met at a dance. They were playing "The Duke of Earl". You know the song. (CLAIRE *is blank.* EPPY *begins to sing shyly.*)

CLAIRE: Was he breast fed?

EPPY: Yes.

CLAIRE: Your breasts are rather small, Eppy. Was it difficult to feed him?

EPPY: Only in the beginning.

CLAIRE: I would like to feed Earl.

EPPY: He's weaned.

CLAIRE: No boy ever weans completely.

EPPY: Your attitude . . .

CLAIRE: My attitude should be your attitude. Am I frightening? Am I rude? Give me a tip on how to flatter you.

EPPY: Keep away from my family, Claire. Please keep away.

CLAIRE: You've every right to fear me. You know we could have traded places years ago. We could have found other names. How was I to know about my own children? I've lost my children along with my husband. It happened like punishment from the sky. Like vultures eating out of my womb. Being molested by brutal monsters from hell. My insides will never be the same.

EPPY: Please leave, Claire.

CLAIRE: Another migraine?

EPPY: Yes. Worse.

CLAIRE: I'll go. Until later then.

EPPY: You needn't.

CLAIRE: Until later, my dear.

END OF SCENE

SCENE TWO

(Same day. Evening at EPPY *and* ARNOLD's *home.* EPPY *maintains her sense of humor during this bout.)*

EPPY: I met her.

ARNOLD: You met who?

EPPY: Claire. The woman you've been flirting with at work.

ARNOLD: Who?

EPPY: Claire. You know. Horror movie make-up, perhaps a collection of cheap mail-order wigs . . . polyester scarves . . .

ARNOLD: Darling, you must be mistaken.

EPPY: She approached me after lunch. Today. *(Pause. Waiting for a reaction)* Did you put her up to it?

ARNOLD: What are you talking about?

EPPY: Little Tootsie with the laser tongue.

ARNOLD: I'm lost at sea, Eppy.

EPPY: Is there something wrong with our marriage?

ARNOLD: No. Of course not.

EPPY: Is there something defective inside me?

ARNOLD: Darling . . .

EPPY: Are we not a pair?

ARNOLD: Did I forget our anniversary?

EPPY: No. I'm talking about this creature Claire.

ARNOLD: Who is she?

EPPY: You told her intimate things.

ARNOLD: Nonsense.

EPPY: I'm not built for this kind of punishment. God-help-us. I'm a frail, insecure woman. If someone shouts, I go to pieces. I'm not equipped to handle shocks. *(Pause)* Where's Earl?

ARNOLD: At the sitter's.

EPPY: Which sitter?

ARNOLD: The Greek woman downstairs.

EPPY: Sitters aren't safe.

ARNOLD: Since when?

EPPY: I'm very frightened, Arnold. *(Pause)* There are child-snatchers everywhere. I think I met one today.

ARNOLD: Darling, come to your senses.

EPPY: You must stop meeting strange women at work.

ARNOLD: Tell my boss.

EPPY: I'm telling you.

ARNOLD: Why are you so suspicious?

EPPY: It's the way you look at other women.

ARNOLD: None are prettier than you, Eppy.

EPPY: She seems to know everything about you. About us. *(Pause)* I know. You'll tell me to ignore her. Call her a simple crank. Dismiss it. I can't.

ARNOLD: Have you ever seen her before?

EPPY: No.

ARNOLD: Are you sure that's her right name?

EPPY: No.

ARNOLD: At any rate, I wouldn't worry so. Gossip travels like lightning in my office. She picked up things from someone at work.

EPPY: She made a crazy request.

ARNOLD: Did she?

EPPY: I refused her.

ARNOLD: Good.

EPPY: Don't you want to know what she asked?

ARNOLD: No. Whatever it was, I'm certain it was destructive.

EPPY: She wants you for a day.

ARNOLD: Why?

EPPY: Take a guess.

ARNOLD: I'm not good at this sort of thing.

EPPY: How do you know Claire?

ARNOLD: I don't.

EPPY: Arnold . . . I don't believe you.

ARNOLD: How unfortunate, Eppy. Love is trust.

EPPY: She will be back.

ARNOLD: This. . . Claire?

EPPY: How did you pass the week?

ARNOLD: Making money for you.

EPPY: Did you work hard, Arnold?

ARNOLD: Yes. In fact I put down a deposit for some farm land. Five-hour drive north. Several hundred acres. I thought we needed a second home. Open country for Earl to explore.

EPPY: A farm?

ARNOLD: Dairy.

EPPY: Did you see the land?

ARNOLD: Yes. Went up with the realtor.

EPPY: When?

ARNOLD: Oh, earlier this month.

EPPY: Why didn't you let me come with you?

ARNOLD: It was to be a surprise.

EPPY: A surprise?

ARNOLD: Did I do something wrong?

EPPY: Did you drive up with this woman?

ARNOLD: Darling, this isn't like you.

EPPY: She wears the strangest perfume.

ARNOLD: You say that about many people.

EPPY: What cold eyes . . . like a reptile in captivity. She kept touching my arm for emphasis. Touching me like I was inferior. Looking at my features for imperfections. I had trouble holding my own. I was frightened. Kept hoping she would be bored with me. Hoping she would fly away without ceremony. (Pause) But I sensed she had your approval. And that's what hurt most.

ARNOLD: You're my wife, Eppy. . . .

EPPY: Haven't I earned your loyalty?

ARNOLD: No one's more loyal. No one loves harder. *(Pause)* No one threatens you. There are many damaged people running around. You mustn't be open to them. I'm a trial lawyer with too many scores set against me. Vendettas a mile long.

EPPY: It is a vendetta.

ARNOLD: Alright. I'll meet this woman and find out.

EPPY: Find out what?

ARNOLD: What the game is.

EPPY: I know the game.

ARNOLD: Do you?

EPPY: I'm not a paranoid, Arnold. I'm not bait for animals on prey. If you're going to meet with her, I want to be present.

ARNOLD: Fine.

EPPY: And I get to cross-examine.

ARNOLD: As you wish.

EPPY: Because she could eat you up in one bite.

ARNOLD: I certainly hope not.

EPPY: Can you be so certain?

ARNOLD: I've great powers of observation. Very few people can fool me. It's in the voice. It's in the movement of the eyes. It's in the hand gesture. Twelve years in the courtroom. I think I know a liar at first sight. *(Pause)* I know the devious game women play. This woman is no different.

EPPY: Tell me something, Arnold.

ARNOLD: What?

EPPY: Should I fear her?

ARNOLD: Claire? *(Pause)* Not at all.

EPPY: And if I'm confused?

ARNOLD: I'll kiss you in public.

EPPY: She's prettier than me.

ARNOLD: It depends on how you wear your hair.

EPPY: She's sexier. Shrewder. A schemer. She knows my weaknesses. I can sense these things. And they feed my anxieties. I see little maneuvers. And I can make a tragic mistake. I mustn't do that. It would kill me so.

END OF SCENE

SCENE THREE

(Three days later. Afternoon. Central Park.)

CLAIRE: Your son is quite handsome. *(Pause)* Do I keep repeating myself? I'm in love with your little boy. I've watched him in the playground many many hours in all kinds of weather. He's the sort of toddler for a poster campaign. He's sweeter than honey. I would adopt him in a moment's notice. That's how strong the connection is. Very penetrating. I can see the resemblance to his father. The decisive brow. The alert eyes. The devilish smile. The magic in the pelvis. *(Pause)* I've said too much.

ARNOLD: No.

CLAIRE: You've been very patient with me.

ARNOLD: Have I?

CLAIRE: Indeed. I hate to monopolize your time.

ARNOLD: I took the afternoon off.

CLAIRE: For me?

ARNOLD: Yes, my wife thought it was important to make this visit.

CLAIRE: She's not the sort of woman I thought you would marry.

ARNOLD: You hardly know me.

CLAIRE: Yes, still I think I have an intuition. A special vision. A hankering for good-looking men. *(Pause)* I asked your wife to have one day with you. Did she tell you?

ARNOLD: Yes.

CLAIRE: Did you think it was a peculiar request?

ARNOLD: Yes, I'd say so.

CLAIRE: Would you mind very much?

ARNOLD: You have to be kidding.

CLAIRE: I'm drawn to you, Arnold. And to little Earl. *(She sings* "Duke of Earl".*)* Come stay with me for the afternoon. My apartment's not far away. I could make a lunch.

ARNOLD: You and I have no common business.

CLAIRE: We do, Arnold.

ARNOLD: What business then?

CLAIRE: I'm lonely. Do you understand such things? *(Pause)* I'm having trouble dating men, you see. I don't know what's happened to my self-confidence. It's quite awful. . . . I can't make silly conversation. Can't flirt at the door. Petrify whenever a man comes to kiss me. *(Pause)* You understand, Arnold.

ARNOLD: No.

CLAIRE: Make love to me, Arnold. Now.

ARNOLD: How's that?

CLAIRE: Make love to me, or let me tell a bedtime story to little Earl.

ARNOLD: Are you out of your mind?

CLAIRE: Is my appetite showing? I didn't mean to appear so. . . so famished. Surely, you've dreamt of me many times. You've injured me, too. Well, our time today can make up for the past. Come, kiss me on the mouth. Openly. With heat. I burn for your time. Please, Arnold, don't deliberate. Touch me here. Give me an emotion. Give me peace.

ARNOLD: I don't think I can help you.

CLAIRE: I want a child.

ARNOLD: Yes, well . . .

CLAIRE: This won't be the first time, I've other family. Maybe I'm exaggerating my needs. Surely you've been to the zoo. The line of perverse monkeys masturbating. . . . Yes, my offspring. My darling creatures. My eccentric legacy. *(Pause)* When I see little Earl in the school yard, I grow excited. The boy excites me. I should have nursed him years ago. *(Pause)* So I am determined to nurse you.

ARNOLD: Is this how you spoke to my wife before?

CLAIRE: I hope she wasn't insulted.

ARNOLD: My wife's an old-fashioned girl.

CLAIRE: Aren't we all?

ARNOLD: As I said, I don't think I can help you. It would be wise not to pursue my family beyond today. You know what I mean. My wife can't cope with shocks. Nor can I. And though you're very attractive, I don't see how we may sleep together in the course of an afternoon from work.

CLAIRE: But the notion did enter your mind?

ARNOLD: You shouldn't have mentioned my son in the same breath.

CLAIRE: I think I'm on a binge. I literally ache for company. I talk to stuffed toys on my bed. Watch the window of the pet store. Cry in my sleep. Yes, Arnold. I'm an unhappy little gal with no loving husband. I haven't seen a male organ in a small eternity. Just to see you urinate with the bathroom door ajar. . . .

ARNOLD: The door must always be shut.

CLAIRE: Not when the two are a couple. . . .

ARNOLD: You act so self-assured.

CLAIRE: Do I? I thought I was fighting shyness. Come, Arnold. Embrace me for a second. We can pretend to be in love. To recall my lost virginity and my oils and easel. My piano. My hope chest. *(Pause)* Impregnate me, Arnold. My cycle is most willing. Ovary yearning.

ARNOLD: Claire, this is too much nonsense.

CLAIRE: Take off my dress, Arnold.

ARNOLD: Don't make a fool of me. My wife is incensed at this intrigue.

CLAIRE: Your wife is inferior.

ARNOLD: Who are you, Claire?

CLAIRE: A suburban witch. A Bohemian bitch. A painter and pianist. What difference does it make, Arnold? Forget my biography. I have. Discover me without a name. How maddening to shed our skins before an affair of the heart. Kiss, kiss, kiss. *(Pause. Mock disciplinary voice.)* Strip to the feet, young man. Do as I say. Or there will be an unfortunate reprisal.

ARNOLD: I need to call a lawyer.

CLAIRE: You are a lawyer.

ARNOLD: You're unrelenting. *(Pause)* I can't stay, Claire. I ask in all civility that you keep away from my wife and home. I won't hesitate in calling the police. You appear to be deeply troubled. I wish I could be of more help. *(Handing her an envelope)* Please. There's enough cash inside to make you obey. I needn't go this far. But I sense a profound loneliness inside you. This isn't charity, but a form of chivalry. If you go away with any impression of me, know that I'm chivalrous. *(Accepts envelope, then kisses him hard on the mouth)*

END OF SCENE

SCENE FOUR

(Three days later. Café.)

EPPY: *(Restrained)* My husband told me everything.

CLAIRE: But you're still upset with me?

EPPY: He gave you a large sum of money.

CLAIRE: And I spent it in one day.

EPPY: We won't give you anything more.

CLAIRE: I massaged his heart and chest. Did he tell you that? Did he tell you that he was feeling extremely faint? That I breathed life into him and applied the Heimlich maneuver after a difficult dessert? *(Pause)* That he bled at the mouth and cried in his sleep? That he was nursed for an hour? Milked and weaned by a perfect stranger from Boston? *(Pause)* That he fell in love with me? That he made damaging remarks about you? That he betrayed your love in him? *(Pause)* That he must betray you.

EPPY: I can't understand your motives.

CLAIRE: My motives are to win your husband, for just
a day. He's not much for endurance. I can sense a
weak heart, a wandering mind. Just a day and he'll
come back to normal. And back to his second wife.
His intended spouse. His high-school sweetheart.
His partner at K Marts.

EPPY: You say this out of envy?

CLAIRE: Out of sweet wickedness and sobriety.

EPPY: You know we phoned the police.

CLAIRE: It won't do you any good. Crimes of passion
slip off the police blotter. *(Pause)* Hasn't your husband
told you about our past? *(Pause)* I guess not.
Well, dear Eppy, shall I make this easy for you to
understand? I was once married to Arnold. *(Pause)*
No. I have no proof. You'll think it's all hearsay.
But we were wedded . . . years ago in full possession
of our faculties. And we had a child. The child died.
Or was stolen by a wicked person. Very hard to
believe? I beg you to listen to me. The child we
bore resembled Earl. I'll stop if this is unbearable.

EPPY: You are unbearable.

CLAIRE: God is against me. Can you understand that,
Eppy? My womb was sewn with steel thread. My
body was an object of derision. My head was shorn
with a dull razor. I was gagged with a rag covered
with morphine. Asleep for thousands of years,
without comfort or protection from the elements.
I was once infinitely more beautiful. I didn't need
clothes. I had many children. But none was more
precious to me than the boy which resembled Earl.
The élan. The golden glow. The boyish smile. Your
son is no stranger to me. We have given birth to the
same magnificent spirit. We are beloved sisters.
We are mothers of a rare angel from Heaven.
Don't cast me away when we share so much common

destiny. Arnold knows this. Forgive his denials. His embarrassment is rather large. Talk to me, Eppy. Give me your God-given warmth.

EPPY: My God-given warmth?

CLAIRE: Give me your bosom, pumpkin.

EPPY: No. Get away. Fly to hell. I hate your coy, ridiculous smile. If you come around again, I'll tear your devilish eyes out. This I do swear!

END OF SCENE

SCENE FIVE

(That evening at home)

EPPY: I'm not loved.

ARNOLD: But you are.

EPPY: I'm not loved enough.

ARNOLD: Says who?

EPPY: I'm falling apart inside. Can't you see that? Why is this happening to me?

ARNOLD: I don't know.

EPPY: It's because of her. It's because of her spells. You've seen her without me.

ARNOLD: Nonsense. I think you're a little confused. And tired.

EPPY: I'm not tired.

ARNOLD: We should have been born into poverty. That would change things. What can I give you now? Diamonds and furs? I bought you a cozy farm. A tractor. An ecologically correct Jacuzzi. What pleases us cannot last very long. Is that my fault?

I promised you to be reliable. A bedrock for our difficult moments, our emotional storms. No woman can take that away from us. No spirit on Earth.

EPPY: She's not from the Earth, Arnold.

ARNOLD: Where is she from?

EPPY: From Mars. From Saturn. From Uranus.

ARNOLD: A commuter?

EPPY: She said she was once your wife.

ARNOLD: How bizarre.

EPPY: Well?

ARNOLD: Well, what?

EPPY: Is she from your past?

ARNOLD: I don't remember.

EPPY: You don't remember?

ARNOLD: Perhaps very very long ago.

EPPY: Did you have an affair with her?

ARNOLD: Does it really matter now?

EPPY: Yes! Why couldn't you have told me before?

ARNOLD: Shyness.

EPPY: You're a compulsive liar. I'll kill her next chance I get.

ARNOLD: Eppy . . .

EPPY: With a very blunt metal instrument.

ARNOLD: The two of you should learn to become friends.

EPPY: Friends? Don't torture me today. Or I'll try to kill you, too. I'm in a killing mood. A gorgeous, black mood. What new blood will spill in our home?

ARNOLD: Don't be gothic.

EPPY: She won't steal Earl.

ARNOLD: She wouldn't stoop to that.

EPPY: How do you know?

ARNOLD: Let me exercise some judgment.

EPPY: But you're a fool half the time.

ARNOLD: Only to amuse you when you're depressed.

EPPY: Arnold, she may just kidnap Earl. Anything's
possible. You must make a clean break, and do it
quickly. Tonight. Or bring in the police. If you want,
I'll be there as a witness. Unless you've a better idea?

ARNOLD: Let's not involve the police. I'll speak to
Claire one last time. I've got guts. I'll wrap it up.
I love you with all my heart.

EPPY: Fine. You make me feel so happy. *(Pause)*
Tonight then.

END OF SCENE

SCENE SIX

(Next day. Evening at EPPY *and* ARNOLD*'s home.* EPPY *is
away.)*

CLAIRE: *(Not looking at* ARNOLD. *He is motionless.)*
Take your shoes off. Take off your trousers. Take off
your shirt and tie. Take off rings and jewelry. Take
down the family photos. Come closer. Leave the
window shades as they are. We're not going into the
room. We're not going to do this like your jejune
Eppy doll. That's how it must be. I'm angry, you see.
I'm going to make you feel rockets of delight. . . if you
permit me. You can watch me. Better to watch me.

Or close your eyes. Pull my hair. I won't feel any
pain tonight. I purchased tonight, you see. I did.
You shouldn't frown so, makes your face look like
a kippered herring. Well, you can approach me now.
I'm ready for anything. I'm carnivorous if you choose
to be consumed. I'm dangerous if you let me roam.
I'm a girl scout with a very pronounced tongue.
I'm a Born Again with dewdrop organs. I'm a
forbidden flower on your guilt-ridden mind. *(Pause)*
Now, Arnold. I can't wait for parades.

ARNOLD: No.

CLAIRE: I own you tonight.

ARNOLD: Not here.

CLAIRE: We're alone. I'll sing to you first. Won't that
help? A song of memory and remorse. A song to
console you. A cherry for your palate. Camphor for
your soul.

ARNOLD: Our union was annulled long ago.

CLAIRE: Our union has just begun, my lovely.

ARNOLD: Where is that light coming from?

CLAIRE: From my hands.

ARNOLD: Put them away.

CLAIRE: The light is to exalt you.

ARNOLD: Assault me.

CLAIRE: Then you must shut your eyes, for I intend to
bathe you clean. My little child. My masculine lover.
My vicious partner in crime. Shut those eyes. Claire
came for you. Came for a particular throbbing. I see
your nervousness. Your fear of fertility. How silly.
Every garden should be fertile. *(Silence)* Remember
the Arabian stallion at sea cliff? The tempestuous
winds against us along the fiords? The torrential

downpour . . . and recalcitrant demons pursuing us?
Galloping and galloping for dear life. The flaming
heat from the stallion. The asthmatic pain we felt.
The welts from the sadistic beatings. The pessimism
from God. I never felt more challenged, my sweet
gondolier. We had passion for strange dark risks.
We had style and defiance. We had animal instinct.
And now, you ask for banalities. Arnold, forget your
name. It's our moment to raise hell. Spit into the
face you really hate. I defy our destiny for want of a
normal offspring. And normal is what I crave, darling.

ARNOLD: A quick fuck.

CLAIRE: How quick?

ARNOLD: Offer me something in exchange.

CLAIRE: What?

ARNOLD: That you'll leave town, never to return.

CLAIRE: Agreed.

ARNOLD: Because my wife will certainly try to kill
you.

CLAIRE: Yes, I know.

ARNOLD: I wouldn't underestimate her.

CLAIRE: She is so wooden, Arnold. So lead-footed.
So . . . wifey.

ARNOLD: Were you much different?

CLAIRE: I don't think you can afford this round of
amnesia.

ARNOLD: With so many better-looking men
everywhere, why continue with me?

CLAIRE: You can't ask that question, Arnold. It's a
violation of our pact.

ARNOLD: Did we have a pact at all?

CLAIRE: Yes.

ARNOLD: Did I sign it?

CLAIRE: Yes. In the presence of angels.

ARNOLD: But I don't remember any angels.

CLAIRE: They were there. Yes indeed. In uniform
white, cotton-puff. A ton of talcum powder.
The angels hoisted us. You fell from dizziness.
You brought fruits and other gifts to the flock of
heaven's staunch soldiers. *(Pause)* Come, don't
burden yourself with these details. We have other
business. Please me, Arnold. Care for me. Envelop
me and keep me from harm. Run away with me.
She won't miss you. If anything, she holds you in
contempt. She's domesticated you. You've a ludicrous
ring between your nose. Pluck the ring, Arnold.
And fuck me to your heart's content.

ARNOLD: Now?

CLAIRE: Yes, now.

ARNOLD: On the floor?

CLAIRE: Wherever.

ARNOLD: Shall I get a blanket first?

CLAIRE: Hurry, Arnold.

ARNOLD: I can't decide what to do.

CLAIRE: Please me.

ARNOLD: Eppy will barge in. I know it.

CLAIRE: There is an amulet at the door. It will keep the
bitch away.

ARNOLD: You believe in magic?

CLAIRE: Yes.

ARNOLD: It won't keep Eppy from the door.

CLAIRE: There are amulets for all occasions. *(Pause)* It's the safe thing to do. Hang a religious article upside down. Besides, she's protecting your son from view. Believing I'm death's messenger. And a child molester. Her fantasies know no bounds. *(Pause)* Or forget the amulet. Let her see us. She'll be more satisfied if she confirmed her fears. Eppy is a masochistic squirrel. Weak wuss woman. A cipher. An insect in an apron.

ARNOLD: You're envious.

CLAIRE: Of her servitude?

ARNOLD: Of her security.

CLAIRE: Don't be ridiculous. I'll start a very nasty fight. Obey me. Down to the floor. Face down. Don't say a word. Or I'll correct you. You won't like that. I keep my shoes on. Did you see my shoes? I must do things my way. It will happen so fast that you won't even notice. Yes, really. So Arnold, take care of yourself and pay strict attention. It's like your bridal night in Philadelphia.

ARNOLD: *(Halting, quiet anguish)* I can't. *(Foreplay stops.)*

END OF SCENE

SCENE SEVEN

(Next day. Sunday afternoon at home.)

EPPY: *(Half ridicule, half anger, cloaked in composure)* When I found you this morning I couldn't believe the condition of your ... your. .... You've changed beyond recognition. I was on my way to church. Where did you go? What did you do? Who did this to you? You're scarred and bruised. You had a sexual

rendezvous. With you-know-who. And you should
be embarrassed. You should be hung dead. I told you
not to see her again. *(Pause)* She stole Earl and left a
note. She promises to return him in a day. That's all
the time she needs. I'm still in shock. This woman has
no heart, just teeth and claws. Utter poison. I'll kill
her. *(Pause)* Call her, Arnold. Tell her to come back to
see you. She'll come. Too brazen to fear an ambush.
I want to give her my regards. Right? Isn't it the
correct thing to do? *(Pause)* Isn't it?

ARNOLD: Yes, Eppy.

END OF SCENE

SCENE EIGHT

(Next day. Central Park.)

EPPY: *(Clutching a child inside a large overcoat, talking
sweetly and optimistically)* I'm going to bathe you. Feed
you. Calm you down. You're hungry, sweetie. I won't
let you alone again. I'm your mother. And I've missed
you so. Did she hurt you? *(Pause)* We thought it
would be hard to find you. We called the police.
But we were lucky. So lucky. Thank the Lord. Your
father thinks she won't come back. He's afraid of her.
I want her to come back. I'm not afraid. I must collect
my debt. I must fight street-style. But I can't leave you
with your father. So get your clothes together and
we'll go tonight. *(Pause)* Mother loves you, darling.
God bless you.

END OF SCENE

SCENE NINE

(Two days later. EPPY *and* ARNOLD's *home. Evening.)*

ARNOLD: I'm at a decisive disadvantage, Claire.
You've maneuvered me into a corner. You've no right
to do this. The police are looking for you. Better pray
they find you before Eppy. She's taken Earl. Gone
somewhere. Don't know where. She left a note.
She blames me for everything. Says you've molested
our boy. Says Earl has little hickeys all over him.
It's one thing to mess with me. But not my little boy.
Don't you know right from wrong? He's not yet ten.
He's not your son. I don't care what you imagine.
Children aren't. . . . I could destroy you for what
you've done. I'm very confused, Claire. Are you
taking revenge on me? My boy shouldn't have to
suffer for the things that I've done. Do you
understand? You were told to leave town. I gave you
money.

CLAIRE: You once loved me, Arnold.

ARNOLD: And if I did?

CLAIRE: Who killed my sons?

ARNOLD: I don't know.

CLAIRE: You do know. How will you protect Earl
from me?

ARNOLD: Claire, it wasn't my fault.

CLAIRE: You can apologize. Make necessary changes.

ARNOLD: You want me to leave her.

CLAIRE: *Severe* changes.

ARNOLD: You want Eppy dead.

CLAIRE: Yes.

ARNOLD: Then do it yourself.

CLAIRE: You must do it.

ARNOLD: I can't. She's my wife.

CLAIRE: Weakling.

ARNOLD: I'll hire someone.

CLAIRE: Tomorrow.

ARNOLD: You get pleasure from this.

CLAIRE: No.

ARNOLD: I can read your face.

CLAIRE: Give me a son, Arnold. That's all I ask.
A child for my old age. A boy who will sleep by me.
Every mother knows this. Because our husbands fail
us, we depend on our legitimate sons. When Mother's
Day arrives. For roses and telegrams. For our bed
linen. In the bath amid the boats and ducks and suds.
I must have your seed. My belly must grow. I must
feel life tunnel through.

ARNOLD: I can sleep with you without hurting Eppy.

CLAIRE: But you give no semen. When you come,
it is confetti, Arnold.

ARNOLD: Let me try.

CLAIRE: You must kill your wife first.

ARNOLD: Come to bed, Claire. I'll whet your appetite.

CLAIRE: Bravado makes you look silly. *(Pause)* Alright
then. Take me to bed. Give me a little dynamite.
I think I deserve it. I've fornicated with bats and
weasels. I've run with wild geese. Swapping partners
for forlorn nightmares. Give me consolation. The
demon nights are bitter. The bitch winds in the

Rockies. The miserable rains in April. Give me
motherly affection. I'm the last moment of grace in
this century. Kiss me now. We are strangers no more.
We are angels in distress. We are in love. We can live
happy in each other's arms. You can impregnate me
like never before. Charge me with white energy. May
we drink as in the old days. Bring me to my knees.

ARNOLD: Get on your knees.

CLAIRE: For you?

ARNOLD: Yes.

CLAIRE: I want top.

ARNOLD: Always top.

CLAIRE: I ride the storm.

ARNOLD: Always the storm.

CLAIRE: I watch out for you.

ARNOLD: Get on your knees.

CLAIRE: Feisty boy.

ARNOLD: You taught me things.

CLAIRE: Have I?

ARNOLD: Evasive action.

CLAIRE: Do I do that?

ARNOLD: And tease a troubled mind.

CLAIRE: I tease you to entertain you.

ARNOLD: Get on your knees.

CLAIRE: Can I trust you?

ARNOLD: Yes.

CLAIRE: Side by side.

ARNOLD: Claire, you want a special prize. A progeny. Do as I say. I want to please you. And get past our problems. You want an animal, but I'm simply a dull husband. I'll try to be an animal. You may have a laugh. But this is what I do best. *(Pause)* I have pride in the endeavour. *(Long, passionate kiss)*

END OF SCENE

SCENE TEN

(EARL on a chair, CLAIRE with an orange for him. The next day, CLAIRE's apartment.)

CLAIRE: Make a big big smile. *(He does.)* What's my name?

EARL: Aunt Claire.

CLAIRE: Do you love me?

EARL: Yes.

CLAIRE: Yes, what?

EARL: Yes, sweet Auntie.

CLAIRE: Did you walk here, or take the bus?

EARL: I walked here. *(Pause)* What did you do with my socks?

CLAIRE: I'm washing them clean. *(Feeds him orange while singing* "Duke of Earl"*)*

EARL: Do my feet smell?

CLAIRE: No, do mine?

EARL: My father says if your feet smell and your nose runs, you're built backwards. Do you like my father? Do you think he's handsome? Do I look like him?

CLAIRE: You do.

EARL: Are you going to wash my hair again?

CLAIRE: If you like.

EARL: But the deal is — no suds.

CLAIRE: No suds, Earl. Give me your hand.
(He extends both hands to her.)

END OF SCENE

SCENE ELEVEN

(The next day. CLAIRE, EPPY *and* ARNOLD *meet together for the first time at* EPPY *and* ARNOLD's.)

CLAIRE: The little boy has the wrong mother. I've told him this. Stupid bitch. His fat little arms and thighs. I do own him. I had once carried him in my belly. Don't talk to me about resemblance. He resembles my lost blessing. *(Pause)* You don't pity me. Not a tear drop. Earl came to me because he wanted to see me again. You can't free your son just yet. You'll have to do as I say.

EPPY: I'll kill you first.

CLAIRE: You haven't the nerve.

ARNOLD: Let's be sensible. *(Experiences chest pain suddenly)*

EPPY: Don't push me, Claire. Where is my boy?

CLAIRE: In my bed.

EPPY: What have you done with him?

CLAIRE: I became his bride.

EPPY: You ugly, perverse witch.

ARNOLD: Eppy! *(More chest pain)*

CLAIRE: Please, you mustn't insult me. I'm very touchy about name-calling.

EPPY: Where's Earl?

CLAIRE: You won't know unless you behave better, Eppy. Smarten up. You want peace of mind. I can give you that. I still have your boy. Taught him sex. Quickly. He knows how to respond like a man. Be proud of him. He moves like a man. Strode tall. Earl's no little boy. And I'm no old lady. The chemistry was, as they say, just right. What Arnold lacks, Earl makes up in spades.

ARNOLD: Ah, shut-up!

CLAIRE: How can I return little Earl without getting something valuable?

EPPY: You're an extortionist, and I can't afford the price.

CLAIRE: Certainly you can.

EPPY: I want my boy.

CLAIRE: Do you deserve him? Can you make him as happy as I can? Do you let him play rough and dirty in the schoolyard?

EPPY: Your intentions are unacceptable.

CLAIRE: Ask Earl.

ARNOLD: Claire, you're a beautiful, misguided woman. Our lives have become hopelessly tangled. I think it's time to return our little boy. Kidnapping is a federal offense. We're talking 15 to 20 years. The police are just a phone call away.

CLAIRE: You wouldn't risk the scandal. I'll charge that you raped me.

EPPY: *(To* ARNOLD*)* You can't reason with her.

ARNOLD: Give her a few minutes.

EPPY: No. What is it?

ARNOLD: My chest . . .

CLAIRE: You look so very miserable, Eppy. Now you know what was done to me.

EPPY: I don't give a damn.

CLAIRE: How about a little solidarity between feminists?

EPPY: If you don't return my son immediately, you leave me no choice. I don't really care what secret powers you possess. I don't care who you really are. And who is behind you. I only want my boy home. Safe and sound. Unmolested. If you're thinking of going further with his stunt. . . I will pity you. You're the woman every woman fears. I did a little research. *(Pause. Produces amulet without fanfare.)* I bought this at the local junk shop. Here. See your likeness. Indulge yourself. Maybe you'll choke on it. The liquid should burn you worse than battery acid. It's up to you. Defend yourself.

CLAIRE: Defend myself?

EPPY: I will stop at nothing.

ARNOLD: Eppy, don't go over your head.

CLAIRE: It's good that you fear me, Eppy. Better to know the worst this world has to offer you. This world was meant for you, but I was born to this world before you. You hate spiders and colony insects. You should find tolerance inside your heart. Put down the amulet. You can turn the other cheek. God will respect you. I do. Eppy, come hold me. I'm an endangered species. My pain overwhelms me. I live through tragedies and ignoble romances. I don't realize all the things I do. Impulses rule me. My heart is pure. As pure as yours. Put away the amulet. Give me respect, Eppy. Earl is safe, I swear. He will be yours again. I promise you.

EPPY: Your promises mean nothing.

CLAIRE: You hardly know me.

ARNOLD: I think she does.

EPPY: I know you exceedingly well.

CLAIRE: Perhaps you do. Our anatomy is rather similar.

EPPY: Only on the surface. Your appearance is a hellish lie.

CLAIRE: I'm a natural female. You're the counterfeit.

EPPY: Let God decide.

CLAIRE: Which God?

EPPY: God in Heaven.

CLAIRE: If you want a true verdict, call all the jurors, darling.

EPPY: You asked Arnold to kill me.

ARNOLD: Eppy!

EPPY: Didn't you?

CLAIRE: Yes, in fact, I did.

EPPY: And you molest innocents.

CLAIRE: Have I been that bad?

EPPY: It's not for me to decide.

ARNOLD: Eppy, my chest . . .

CLAIRE: *(Watching* EPPY *remove the cap over the vial of liquid)* Go ahead, darling. Play God. Complete your action. I know what you're capable of doing. You can out-play me in violence. The only difference, *darling,* is you are favored by the powers that be. My party is out, until the next election. So, torment me with your defensive amulet charm. Yes, it causes me a dull pain in my heart. Saps my strength. Brings you back your son. *(Takes out* EARL's *clothes from her handbag)* Though this time, you may not recognize him. Here are his clothes. *(Looks at* EPPY *with disdain)* This gave me what I needed. Possession for a new generation. A young male who will continue to dream about me. Who will worship me all the while pretending to be good for you. Who will confuse mother and whore most absently. Thank you, sweet Eppy, for allowing me to enter your home. *(Walks up to* EPPY. EARL *appears, off in the distance.)* Come, kiss me goodbye. When we next meet, my hair will be a shade different, my lips a different hue. When we next meet, you may give me a degree of sympathy. For you've inherited the garden, and I've the restless heart. *(Now within inches of* EPPY*)* You are so beautiful, Eppy. Know that I envy you from a distance.

EPPY: Do you?

CLAIRE: Oh, I do. I know it's irrational. And how I wish I could deny it. Kiss me, Eppy. End my hurt.

EPPY: Get away from me.

CLAIRE: Then I'll kiss you. *(Coming closer. For a moment,* EPPY *is caught in* CLAIRE's *spell. Their lips touch for a long moment. Slowly* EPPY *recoils and throws the liquid in* CLAIRE's *face.)* Bitch! *(Covers her face with her hands for several moments. Lights dim as we see an austere mask covering* CLAIRE's *face. Lights radiate from* CLAIRE's *hands. Her arms slowly extend as if wings in the air.* ARNOLD *and* EARL *are momentarily transfixed, staring at* CLAIRE.*)*

END OF PART TWO AND PLAY